Barbara Barcellos
Gabriela C Carneiro
Evandro S Andrade

Public health implementation in indigenous women

AF155428

Barbara Barcellos
Gabriela C Carneiro
Evandro S Andrade

Public health implementation in indigenous women

An integrative review

ScienciaScripts

Publisher:
Sciencia Scripts
is a trademark of
Dodo Books Indian Ocean Ltd. and OmniScriptum S.R.L publishing group

120 High Road, East Finchley, London, N2 9ED, United Kingdom
Str. Armeneasca 28/1, office 1, Chisinau MD-2012, Republic of Moldova, Europe
Printed at: see last page
ISBN: 978-620-6-24946-7

PUBLIC HEALTH IMPLEMENTATION IN INDIGENOUS WOMEN
: AN INTEGRATIVE REVIEW.

CONTENTS

PUBLIC HEALTH IMPLEMENTATION IN INDIGENOUS WOMEN: AN INTEGRATIVE REVIEW.

BARCELLOS, Barbara.
MONTEIRO, Christina, Mayara.
CARNEIRO, Gabriela Costa.

SUMMARY

Introduction: It is estimated that there are about 5,000 indigenous peoples in the world today, totalling more than 370 million people. In the historical context of indigenous health, the issue has faced major transitions. In 2007, a specific Coordination was created within the indigenous organisation FUNAI to deal with the issues of indigenous women. Objective: To describe through the literature the health care of the indigenous woman. Methodology: This is an integrative review research. Data collection took place between the months of September 2017 and November 2017. The survey of bibliographic data was adopted from the Virtual Health Library (VHL), using the electronic databases: SCIELO, BDENF and LILACS. The following descriptors were used: Indigenous Health; Women's Health; Indigenous Woman and Health Care of the Indigenous Woman. 50 articles were selected, after careful reading only 8 articles remained, 7 in Portuguese and another in Spanish. Resultados y Discusión: When one investigates on a theme that is always approached, but never really manages to treat and care for this people, due to their culture and beliefs, it is quite a challenge. The indigenous people always prefer to treat pathologies acquired through hierbas, rituals or other types of beliefs. Conclusion: Women and the indigenous people in their totality need more preventive care, that is, they need health teams to come to them more often to carry out the preventive care that each gender needs.

Palabras clave: Mujer Indigena; la cultura; Creencias, Atención Preventiva.

SUMMARY

Introduction: It is estimated that there are approximately 5,000 indigenous peoples in the world today, totalling more than 370 million people. In the historical context of indigenous health, the issue has faced major transitions. In 2007, a specific Coordination was created within the indigenous body FUNAI to deal with indigenous women's issues. **Objective: To** describe through the literature the health care of indigenous women. **Methodology:** This is an integrative review type research. Data collection was carried out between the months of September 2017 and November 2017. The survey of bibliographic data was adopted from the Virtual Health Library (VHL), using the electronic databases: SCIELO, BDENF and LILACS. The following descriptors were used: Indigenous Health; Women's Health; Indigenous Woman and Indigenous Women's Health Care. Fifty articles were selected, after a thorough reading only 8 articles remained, 7 in Portuguese and 1 in Spanish. **Results and Discussion:** When researching a topic that is always addressed, but never really able to treat and care for this people, due to their culture and belief is quite a challenge. The indigenous people will always prefer to treat pathologies acquired through herbs, rituals or other types of beliefs. **Conclusion:** Women and indigenous people as a whole need more preventive attention, that is, they need health teams to go to them more often to perform the preventive care that each gender needs.

Keywords: Indigenous Women; Culture; Beliefs; Preventive Care.

I.   INTRODUCTION

It is estimated that there are approximately 5,000 indigenous peoples in the world today, totalling more than 370 million people[1] . A demographic curve was observed in the 1980s and, since then, the indigenous population in the country has grown steadily, indicating a demographic recovery on the part of most of these peoples, although some of these peoples are threatened with extinction[2] . There is a list prepared by ISA (Instituto Sociambiental) which shows that there are tribes that live with 5 to 40 individuals. There are 254 peoples in the list, 48 of which have part of their population residing in other country(ies). According to the 2010 IBGE census, these peoples total 896,917 people[1, 2]. Of these, 324,834 live in cities and 572,083 in rural areas, which corresponds to approximately 0.47% of the country's total population. Indigenous peoples are spread throughout the Brazilian territory. Several of these peoples also inhabit neighbouring countries. In Brazil, the vast majority of indigenous communities live on collective lands, declared by the federal government for their exclusive usufruct, which are the so-called Indigenous Lands (TIs), totalling 711[1] . In the states of the Brazilian Legal Amazon, the population of indigenous people, according to the 2010 IBGE Census, is 433,363 (adding the states of Acre, Amapá, Amazonas, Mato Grosso, Pará, Rondônia, Roraima and Tocantins and Maranhão - disregarding that only part of Maranhão is Legal Amazon)[1] .

In the historical context of indigenous health, the issue has faced major transitions. Around 1910, the health care of indigenous peoples was under the responsibility of the Indian Protection Service (SPI). In this sense, indigenous health care began to have greater assistance from the State, and the recovery of indigenous health in the face of epidemics that emerged at that time was one of the first actions of the State[2] . In August 2010, the Special Secretariat for Indigenous Health (SESAI) was created The creation of a specific secretariat for Indigenous Health resulted in the transfer of actions to the Ministry of Health. It is the responsibility of this Secretariat to coordinate and execute the management process of the Indigenous Health Care Subsystem throughout the National Territory, with the protection, promotion and recovery of the health of indigenous peoples as its responsibility, in line with the public policies and programmes established by the Unified Health System (SUS)[3] .

In 2007, a specific Coordination was created within the indigenous body FUNAI to deal with indigenous women's issues, currently called the Coordination of Gender, Generational Affairs and Mobilisation[1] . From 2008 to 2010, FUNAI organised 13 (thirteen) Regional Participatory Seminars on the Maria da Penha Law, with the participation of 457 (four hundred and fifty-seven) indigenous women representing a total of 139 (one hundred and thirty-nine) ethnic groups. As a conclusion to these seminars, in 2010, the National Meeting of Indigenous Women for the Protection and Promotion of their Rights took place[2] .

There are mismatches in the dialogues between the Brazilian state and indigenous women on the issue of domestic violence[3] . Perhaps because of the restriction on access to tribes due to their culture[3] . Domestic violence is not related to an ethnic and cultural problem, but to the assimilation of non-indigenous practices and elements that have caused an internal disruption in these peoples and therefore distrust of state intervention to solve this problem [4]. Often indigenous men themselves use the discourse of traditional practice in order not to discuss the discrimination that occurs internally in their peoples [4].

In relation to the specificity of indigenous women's health, it is observed that indigenous women seek their independence, conquering their space in society and, little by little, including themselves in social movements due to their needs[3, 5]. There is a high fertility rate among these women, and it may be the result of socio-cultural valorisation, a fact that is evidenced by the significant number of these women being involved in conjugal unions and by the beginning of their sexually reproductive life around the age of 13 that extends until 45. In addition to high fertility rates, there is also an increase in sexually transmitted diseases, gynaecological injuries and mastopathy.

These populations do not usually open up these issues to health professionals, when they do get in touch, or even when indigenous women seek health services. According to some authors, even issues such as prenatal care and childbirth are usually not in demand, as they prefer to keep them under their own control. The need for a differentiated treatment for this portion of the population and the need for training of professionals for specific care is explicit[5] .

a. CHARACTERISATION OF INDIGENOUS PEOPLES

No one knows for sure how indigenous peoples originated on the American continent, but it is known that this continent was occupied around 15 to 25 thousand years ago by peoples from the Asian continent, where they managed to enter the continent through the Bering Strait, in the extreme north of the continent (SANTOS *et al.*, 2008).

As the millennia passed, these people occupied the entire American continent, creating strategies for managing natural resources to protect themselves, making the culture one of the main socio-cultural heritage of the world (KABAD; PÍCOLI; ARANTES, 2011, p. 26).

Through the passage of millennia it was necessary to conceptualise all peoples, and indigenous peoples would not be different, explanations were elaborated through socio-anthropological knowledge and relations throughout history with colonizers of different nations (KABAD; PÍCOLI; ARANTES, 2011, p. 26). The UN (United Nations Organisation) defined indigenous peoples as follows:

> "Indigenous communities, peoples or nations are those who, presenting a continuity with pre-colonial societies that developed in their territories in the past, consider themselves different from other segments that currently predominate in these territories, or in part of them. They constitute non-dominant segments of society and express a commitment to preserve and develop their cultures and transmit to future generations their ancestral territories, their ethnic identities, based on their continued existence as peoples, in accordance with their cultural patterns, social institutions and legal systems".

According to the Indian Statute (Law no. 6001 of 19 December 1973) *"Indian"* is defined by the following collocation:

> Any individual of pre-Columbian origin and ancestry who identifies and is identified as belonging to an ethnic group whose cultural characteristics distinguish it from national society. (BRASIL, 1973. Article 3).

The indigenous communities were the ones that suffered most from the colonisation of the Portuguese in Brazil, due to slavery, infectious diseases that they were not used to, with the obligation to convert to the Catholic religion, in addition to having to change their entire culture because of the Portuguese colonisers (COSTA, 2016; BERBNARDES, 2011; SILVA; DIAZ; SILVA 2011).They have always been peoples who differed from each other, by culture, religion, subsistence, communication and especially by their social organisations (SANTOS *et al*, 2008).They thought that over the years and decades these peoples would stop segregation and would become part of modern civilisation, making culture, politics and social organisation just one. But none of this happened and the Brazilian government saw the need to create ideologies and targeted public policy, with the Federal Constitution of 1988 came more visible rights for the *"Indians"*. *According to* the Constitution, the peoples who were called Indians from that moment on would no longer be forced to assimilate non-indigenous culture.

> *"Indians are recognised as having their social organisation, customs, languages, beliefs and traditions, and original rights over the lands they traditionally occupy, and it is the responsibility of the Union to demarcate, protect and enforce all their property"* *(Brazil, 1988, Article 231).*

Source:<https://www.google.com.br/url?sa=i&source=images&cd=&cad=rja&uact=8&ved=2ahUKEwiG -fn-iuvcAhUHIJAKHR1OCMgQjRx6BAgBEAU&url=http%3A%2F%2Fg1.globo.com%2Fmato-grosso%2Fnoticia%2F2015%2F01%2Fpopulacao-indigena-de-mt-aumenta- quase-50-em-uma-decada.html&psig=AOvVaw2BpDu_QthUgNS62NDE64dP&ust=1534286009278082>

From the moment that the Indians were free to live according to their culture, Brazil took a very important step towards valuing cultures and even more valuing its native people. When a country values culture it values its people. Even if there is still resistance in some places it was already an important step.

b. INDIGENOUS PUBLIC HEALTH POLICIES IN BRAZIL

In 2009, a census was carried out which identified that there are between 257 and 350 million indigenous people in the world. In Latin America alone there are around 400 indigenous peoples, totalling 10% of the population of this region, the most worrying thing is that the mortality rate is 3 to 4 times higher than national averages, especially when we talk about infectious diseases (CENTRO BRASILEIRO DE ANÁLISE E PLANEJAMENTO, 2009).

In Brazil there are around 230 known indigenous peoples located in different regions of the national territory, where there are around 580 thousand indigenous inhabitants and who speak more than 180 distinct languages (PAGLIARO; AZEVEDO; SANTOS, 2005).

The largest concentrations of indigenous population are in the state of Amazonia and the state of Mato Grosso do Sul, where it is the second state with the largest indigenous population in Brazil, leading to a greater demand on health services for specific populations, since the epidemiological profile is different from non-indigenous population (KABAD; PÍCOLI; ARANTES, 2011, p. 23).

Indigenous peoples have been constituted on the margins of society, due to the reduction of their reserves, precarious access to health services and contact with the context foreign to their daily lives, especially villages close to urban centres (SILVA; DIAZ; SILVA, 2015).

According to Santos et al. (2008) only towards the end of the 20th century that Brazilian policies came to really care about indigenous health. So that they could have the right to health in Brazil took a long time, because until the year 1910, there were no public policies aimed at indigenous populations, only non-routine care made by missionaries (BERNARDES, 2011). The responsibility of the Indian Protection Service (SPI) was to guarantee indigenous health care, and the recovery of indigenous health in the face of epidemics that emerged at that time was one of the first actions of the State (BRASIL, 2002).

The National Indian Foundation (FUNAI), created in 1967 to replace the former Indian

Protection Service, which had been created in 1910, and linked to the Ministry of Justice, is the body that takes care of the protection of indigenous rights and the process of recognition, demarcation and homologation of their lands.

Although FUNAI was created only to guarantee rights, in the beginning this body took care of services aimed at improving indigenous health, the teams were called Volante Health Teams (EVS), they served to provide primary health care services for all indigenous peoples (KABAD; PÍCOLI; ARANTES, 2011, p. 33).

Even through all the means of public policy for indigenous health are willing to work we still have to improve it a lot so that all data are reliable, and with means that can respect above all the integrity of each of the indigenous peoples of Brazil.

The growing indigenous social movements in the 1970s produced important changes in the relationship between the State and indigenous peoples and, with this, in the course of indigenous public policies (KABAD; PÍCOLI; ARANTES, 2011, p. 28).

In view of the disorders presented daily over the years by this people, it was essential to create measures that would improve the functioning and capacity to serve the indigenous ethnic group, in order to meet all the guidelines and principles stipulated by the SUS (Unified Health System), thus meeting universality, equity, participation and social control, but for this to be elaborated effectively and efficiently, their culture and epidemiologies must be taken into account (NATIONAL HEALTH FOUNDATION, 2003).

Through this decree it was stipulated that those with Indians would be the sole responsibility of FUNASA - National Health Foundation - and as for the control of these responsibilities it would be up to the District Councils of Indigenous Health (Condisi), Special Indigenous Health Districts (Dsei), Secretariat of Health Care (SAS) of the Ministry of Health, State Secretariats (SES) and Municipal Health Secretariats (SMS) to participate effectively.

The quality of indigenous health care still has many issues to be taken into account (GUIMARÃES, 2011). With access for all in mind, the Brazilian government created the National Programme for the Health Care of Indigenous Peoples (PNASPI) in 2002 (COSTA *et al*, 2016). According to Brazil (2007) all financial resources would be provided by the Brazilian government:

> *"Regarding financial resources for indigenous health, on 17 October 2007, the incentives for basic and specialised indigenous health care were regulated through Ordinance No. 2,656, with the aim of establishing control mechanisms for financial transfers to the municipality and the state in order to 'agree on care for indigenous*

people, strengthening social control over benefits and expenses'" (BRASIL, 2007, pg. 5).

With this came the implementation of the Specialised Indigenous Health Districts - DSEI (GUIMARÃES, 2011; COSTA *et al*, 2016). The DSEI aims to decentralise the teams of basic health units within the villages, so that their treatment is more effective. It is funded by the Brazilian Ministry of Health and is under the responsibility of the National Health Foundation, also known as FUNASA (SANTOS *et al*, 2008).

Within the DSEI, multidisciplinary health teams are taken to the villages to ensure access to health for all, these teams are known as EMSI, that is, Multidisciplinary Indigenous Health Team (COSTA *et a.*, 2016).

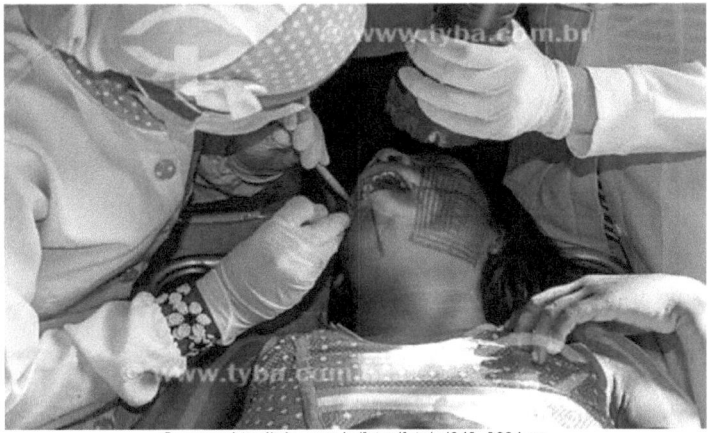

Source:< http://tyba.com.br/fotos/foto/cd343_369.jpg>

This Indigenous Health Care Subsystem, in addition to being organised with DESEI, is also organised in health posts in indigenous lands, Indigenous Sanitation Agents (Aisan), Multiprofessional Indigenous Health Teams (EMSI) and the Casa do Índio (Casai), guiding medium and high complexity services for the SUS network (GUIMARÃES, 2011).

According to Costa *et al* (2016), the structuring of this team is also that of the health team of the Family Health Strategy (ESF), but the denominations are different, that is, there is AIS, which are equivalent to community health agents (ACS), the difference is that the AIS must be a member of the tribe or indigenous community.

Figure 1. Differentiated care

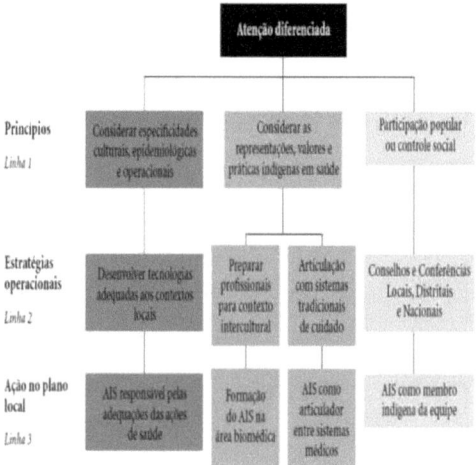

Source: COSTA et al., 2016 *apud* PONTES, REGO E GARNELO, 2015.

This model has shown how important it is to emphasise the policy of respecting the culture of the indigenous people so that an efficient and effective health prevention, promotion and recovery plan can be developed.

There are still many challenges in indigenous primary health care to achieve the long-awaited integrality and equity, especially regarding universal access to health services, integrality of actions and the health care model (CENTRO BRASILEIRO DE ANÁLISE E PLANEJAMENTO, 2009, p.14).

The health actions that give life to this model must be organised to address the problems that arise at the territorial level and these must become parameters to guide health practices, in a continuous way, in locus, but also addressing specific, singular interventions (GUIMARÃES, 2011).It is necessary that public policies focus on the specific needs of each of the indigenous groups, Brazil is a very extensive country, it is not possible to expect standardisation, the regions must always think of a way to organise the treatment of these people, making the demand for health services fair for all, thus working on equity of access and the integrality of health care for all.

In addition, while the world population is getting older, that is, it is decreasing the number of children and getting older, the indigenous population has been growing, as fertility and birth rates are expanding (CENTRO BRASILEIRO DE ANÁLISE E PLANEJAMENTO, 2009).In 2010, the Secretariat of Indigenous Health (SESAI) was created, which resulted in the transfer of specific actions from the Ministry of Health to SESAI, which is responsible for coordinating and executing the management process of the indigenous health care subsystem throughout Brazil, taking into account the prevention, promotion and recovery of health, respecting all the guidelines and principles of SUS (BRASIL, 2009).

c. THE CULTURE OF INDIGENOUS HEALTH

Costa *et al* (2016), says that knowledge in indigenous health legitimises what is most native and ancestral in Brazilian culture and reveals the importance of ancient practices, which do not depend on the imposition of new cultures, methods considered more effective and modern.

When covering the subject of indigenous health, it should be considered that each indigenous people has its ethnicity, way of acting, demographic characteristics and the main its culture and this can modify the ways of interacting with health.

The Indian always had a way to take care of their ailments, but with colonisation came diseases never known before and failed to control their means of contamination, thus causing a spread of some pathologies and causing death of several natives (VERANI, 2011).

Infectious diseases are one of the main causes of death of this people, and chronic non-communicable diseases have been taking an uncontrolled proportion (SANTOS, 2008; VERANI, 2011). In children, respiratory diseases and diarrhoea cause many deaths (NATIONAL HEALTH FOUNDATION, 2003 and 2006). According to the National Health Foundation (2008), each indigenous village organises its health within the territory in an integrated and hierarchical manner, always taking into account the local culture and the principles and guidelines of the SUS. As much as the DSEI teams want to work continuously and be effective, inequality is visible within the service, but this is not for political reasons, it is often due to the location of certain villages, where health teams can only access by boat or plane, as they are located in forests around rivers, among other difficulties.

Source:<https://uploads.metropoles.com/wp-content/uploads/2018/02/09190703/caiuailustracao-840x560.jpg>

The health professional must be aware that when he is attending this specific people he must work both the traditional health environment and the empirical form of indigenous culture, not forgetting that alternative therapies will always be welcome for knowledge, in addition to much of the medicines currently used within the large pharmaceutical networks are because of indigenous knowledge.

In addition to the health professional wanting to gain the trust of the "Indian", the AIS is extremely important, as it makes this link with the health professional who takes care of that particular indigenous village, the AIS brings to the tribes a confidence that what is being offered is really safe and makes individuals with any pathology not abandon the treatment for their cure (GUIMARÃES, 2011).

Religious or health leaders in an indigenous tribe are very strong figures and opinion leaders in front of their people, as they are used in emergency moments, whether or not they have EMSI. These authorities should be highlighted, respected and listened to by health professionals to enable the creation of positive links with the community and avoid conflicts arising from divergent views in the processes of illness and healing (COSTA *et al,* 2016).

When covering the subject of health and how is the culture of indigenous health is necessary to know mainly about the epidemiological profile d this group, because there is precariousness in the information system of morbidity and mortality that are always partial data, never data that can be said to be correct (GUIMARÃES, 2011).

They also face other problems that affect their health as a whole, for example: dispersion of small groups of this population, deprivation of land and dispute over its demarcation or expansion, ecological, cultural changes, and especially contact with society that brings new habits of life, which lead to drastic consequences such as hunger and epidemics of the *"white man"* (GUIMARÃES, 2011).

The tribes that have a larger territory are more likely to have a quality of health both empirical (which they themselves practice on a daily basis) and traditional health with the teams carrying out prevention, promotion and health recovery.

In addition, to assist in health care, indigenous health centres were created, which are a reference network for the care of indigenous people and their companions, where the indigenous individual stays until he has finished his treatment and can return to his village. They are located in reference municipalities or in the capitals of the states (FUNDAÇÃO NACIONAL DE SAÚDE, 2008).

When dealing with indigenous health, differentiated care, in which the culture, epidemiology and operational specificities of these peoples must be considered, since they retain their culture and dialect, as well as their traditions in relation to health-disease (SILVA; DIAZ; SILVA, 2015).

Health actions aimed at this portion of the population must consider the particularities of their culture to achieve the proposed objectives, since these individuals live on the margins of society, isolated within their own universe that must be respected (SILVA; DIAZ; SILVA, 2015).

d. INDIGENOUS WOMEN'S HEALTH

Despite all forms of health care for indigenous peoples, it is still a minority population, representing around 0.4% of the total population of Brazil, indigenous women are still the most vulnerable within this population group, especially in relation to health service care and preventive examinations (PEREIRA et al., 2014).

The means of health policy that assist in this care are not yet 100% effective, due to the fact that no epidemiological data on health conditions are integral, they are always partial.

Health promotion aims to carry out health interventions that focus on the process of health and illness of the subject and their community (PEREIRA et al., 2014).

Indigenous women suffer from violence at all times, mainly because of situations that change their social organisations, loss of territory, the rupture of social, political, economic, religious and health ties that make them more vulnerable (SALES, 2016).

Source:< http://franciscanasdedillingen.org.br/images/galeria/2096/SAM_4188.jpg>

As indigenous women are at risk with regard to their sexual and reproductive health, health promotion strategies that meet their needs and cultural specificities should be prioritised (PEREIRA et al., 2014).

The vast majority of indigenous women start their sex lives early, in some cases women even started sexual intercourse before menarche, but indigenous women are very withdrawn to expose their sexual intimacies to talk about the number of partners, whether they use condoms, it is usually very common to have partner exchanges within the villages (PEREIRA et al., 2014).

Women are very exposed to sexually transmitted infections and diseases due to lack of access to prevention content, increased contact with urban areas, prostitution, use of licit and illicit drugs.

They begin the reproductive period around 11 to 13 years and only ends around 44 years, indigenous women have around 8 to 9 children, even surpassing the level of the national average of non-indigenous women which is 1.9 children per woman (PAGLIARO; AZEVEDO, 2008).

Indigenous women are exposed to risk factors for cervical cancer, have little access to information and preventive examinations, and have a high prevalence of precursor lesions for this type of cancer (PEREIRA *et al.*, 2014).

Due to all the social and demographic problems that the indigenous people suffer daily, it is extremely important to have a vision that covers women in all aspects, the integral look, the human look for them, so that they can plan quality care understanding all the specific needs.

Source: <https://jornalggn.com.br/blog/vicente-estephanio-filho/a-saude-da-mulher-indigena-no-centro-dos-debates>.

Indigenous women want their independence, conquering their space in society and, gradually, including themselves in social movements due to their needs (CRUZ, 2003). They, in general, form a group quite susceptible to the development of pathologies and nutritional deficiencies, due to physiological and hormonal changes that occur during life (BRASIL, 2009).

It is necessary to pay special attention to this group of people, so that a quality of life can be guaranteed for them, through preventive measures, consequently there will be a reduction in diseases. And the most important will be found axis that links their health with their cultural values, which have always been devalued.

The discrimination of issues directly linked to indigenous women involves a critique of State action and the formulation of proposals for new public policies that focus on indigenous women (NETO; SILVA, 2014).

e. THE QUALITY OF HEALTH PROFESSIONAL CARE FOR INDIGENOUS PEOPLE

When talking about quality we can think of different types, never forgetting that what is quality for one may not be for another.

Quality is defined by the Aurélio dictionary:

> "1. good or bad way of being of a thing; 2. superiority, excellence; 3. aptitude, happy disposition; 4. talent, good predicates; 5. title, category; 6. that which characterises a thing; 7. character, nature; 8. caste, species; 9. social, civil, legal condition; 10. Attribute, modality, virtue, value; 11. set of phonetic attributes (pitch, intensity, manner of articulation, timbre) that characterise a given vowel sound; 12. in the capacity of: by way of, with the status of; 13. quality of life: set of conditions for the well-being of an individual or groups of individuals."

Quality was also seen by different management scholars as a tool for companies to stand out from competitors in the business world.

However, when we talk about quality in health professional care we have to take into account the different spheres of this area so rich and that must have quality at all times.

The quality of a health service is based on the idea that it is the treatment offered by a doctor or any other health professional who provides care (ARAUJO et al., 2008).

Health professionals think of quality as being a fundamental part of the process of bringing benefits to their patient's health (ARAUJO et al, 2008), which in a way they are not wrong, bringing benefits to the client's health is an essential part of good quality care, However, it is no use just taking care of the patient's pathology, we have to think about comprehensive care, because as much as "I" as a professional is leading to improvements in the face of his illness, I am not thinking about my patient as a whole if he is worried, if I asked if he was well not in relation to illness, but in relation to himself.

Araújo (2008) says that the professional only provides a quality service if he was really humanised from beginning to end. The worker in this area is evaluated at all times by their patients, how is attention to the client, how interacts, if he follows standards, even if he is recording everything the way it is being reported (TANAKA; ESPÍRITO SANTOS, 2008).

Source:< https://cimi.org.br/wp-content/uploads/2018/04/00MatheusAlvesMNI.jpeg>

One way for the professional to always have a level of quality in care is through training, because it is always good for professionals to develop their techniques no matter how many times they have done it. Permanent and continuing education is an excellent way to always be training and improving quality within a health unit.

The Family Health Strategy (FHS) has quality due to the fact that it is the first step towards successful prevention, through which the number of morbidity and mortality can be drastically reduced.

With the growth of the indigenous people in territories close to the urban area is a reality that demands from the health services a differentiated care, which respects the diversity Inter ethnic of indigenous peoples (PEREIRA et al., 2014).

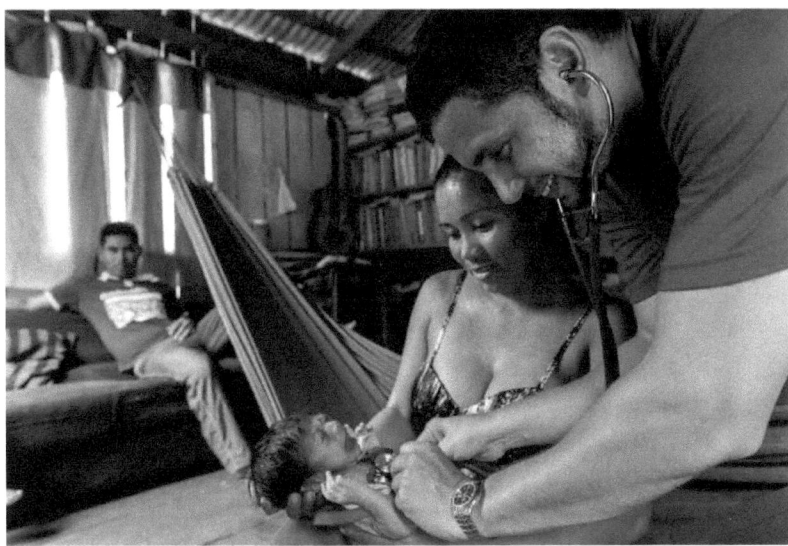

Within indigenous health it would be no different when the multidisciplinary team really cares about care, in seeking to understand each one for their individuality within the indigenous villages everything ends up being worked in the best possible way. And it brings success in the fight against communicable or non-communicable diseases.

If the team is prepared to serve this population in the best possible way, the cost that the government would have during treatment and all other means for recovery of the individual's health will not have, thus increasing the quality of life of the indigenous people and offering a right offered to them at all times, through various articles and statutes.

II.   OBJECTIVE

Describe indigenous women's health care through the literature.

III.   **METHODOLOGY**

a. **Type of Study:**

This is an integrative review type research, which includes the analysis of relevant research that supports decision-making and the improvement of clinical practice, is a type of research developed based on material already elaborated consisting mainly of books and scientific articles. This enables *the synthesis of the state of knowledge of a given subject, in addition to pointing out gaps in knowledge that need to be filled by conducting new studies*[8] .

The integrative review adapts relevant data from a given context to health professionals, keeping them up to date and facilitating changes in clinical practice as a result of research. It is a valuable method for nursing, as professionals often do not have time to read all the available scientific knowledge. The chosen methodology was adopted in this study because it allows the construction of a broad analysis of the researched literature, and allows us to identify where there is a deficiency of studies related to the social exclusion of women who are in a street situation for an improvement in the practice of professionals[8] .

This type of review carefully followed six steps: elaboration of the guiding question; definition of the characteristics of the primary research in the sample; selection of the research that made up the review sample; analysis of the findings of the articles included in the review; interpretation of the results and reporting of the review, which provided critical examination of the findings.

Step 1: Guiding Question:

For the realisation of this article, the guiding question or hypothesis was formulated to define the inclusion and exclusion criteria of the study.

Through this research the answer to be answered: How do indigenous women take care of their personal health, through indigenous culture or through health?

Second Stage: Criteria for Inclusion and Exclusion of Studies:

The articles should have the following inclusion criteria for the integrative review: Address the theme of indigenous women's health care and how it may or may not help indigenous women's health, articles published in Portuguese and Spanish, published in the last fifteen years (2002 to 2017), must be available for free online access and free and complete. Articles that do not answer the guiding question and do not meet the inclusion criteria will be excluded.

Step Three: Definition of the Information to be Extracted from the Studies/Data Collection.

Data collection was carried out between September 2017 and November 2017. The bibliographic data collection was adopted from the Virtual Health Library (VHL), using the electronic databases: Scientific Electronic Library Online (SCIELO), Nursing Database (BDENF), Latin American and Caribbean Literature in Health Sciences (LILACS), in order to gather specific information relevant to the research and reliability of the data contained in the journals.

The following descriptors were used: Indigenous Health; Women's Health; Indigenous Women and Indigenous Women's Health Care. In this way it is considered that it can achieve the objective to find the guiding question and this article.

With the descriptor Indigenous Health, a total of 12,932 articles were found by the VHL, 5784 of which were complete articles, 1032 in Portuguese and 1000 in Spanish. In LILACS 1119 articles were found, 579 complete, 569 in Portuguese and 466 in Spanish. In BDENF 52 articles were found, 35 complete articles, 47 in Portuguese and 3 in Spanish. In SCIELO a total of 484 articles were found, 388 in Portuguese and 58 in Spanish. With the descriptor Women's Health, a total of 30,887 full articles were found by the VHL, 10,122 in Portuguese and 5,430 in Spanish. In LILACS, 8,662 articles were found, 4707 full articles, 5690 in Portuguese and 2333 in Spanish. In BDENF a total of 2,003 articles were found, of which 1,354 were complete articles, 1918 in Portuguese and 80 in Spanish. In SCIELO a total of 2598 articles were found, 2268 in Portuguese and 163 in Spanish.

With the descriptor Indigenous Woman, a total of 376 articles were found by the VHL, of which 145 were complete articles, 73 in Portuguese and 66 in Spanish. In LILACS there are 84 articles,

47 complete, 47 in Portuguese and 36 in Spanish. In BDENF there are 8 articles, 5 of which are complete articles, 8 in Portuguese. In SCIELO a total of 35 articles, 24 in Portuguese and 7 in Spanish. With the descriptor Health care for indigenous women, 40 articles were found by the BVS, 22 of which were complete, 13 in Portuguese and 1 in Spanish. In LILACS a total of 10 articles, 9 complete, 9 in Portuguese and 1 in Spanish. In BDENF a total of 3 articles being all complete and in Portuguese. In SCIELO no article was found with this descriptor. Fifty articles were selected, after a thorough reading only 8 articles remained, 7 in Portuguese and 1 in Spanish.

Fourth stage: Evaluation of the studies included in the review:

After a careful reading of the selected articles, a table will be completed containing: title of the publication, authors, language and country of the article, objective and year. The issues of methodology, outcome and interventions carried out in the publication will be discussed in the results.

Step Five: Interpretation of Results:

This stage corresponds to the discussion phase of the main results in the conventional research. This stage consists of the synthesis, discussion and comparison of the main results obtained by reading the articles and filling in the instrument used.

Step 6: Presentation of the Review/Data:

The integrative review should contain information so that any reader can identify the relevance of this study. All the results and discussion of the data were distributed and organised in charts and tables, all based on the theoretical framework.

IV.   RESULTS AND DISCUSSION

After a thorough search, the data obtained will be presented. The first table shows the titles and analyses of the chosen studies.

ARTICLE NO.	ARTICLE TITLE	AUTHOR(S)	YEAR OF PUBLICATION	LANGUAGE AND	OBJECTIVE
1	Prevalence of diabetes mellitus associated factors in indigenous women from the municipality of Dourados, Mato Grosso do Sul, Brazil.	Freitas G A, Souza MCC, Lima RC	2016	Portuguese/ Brazil	Estimate prevalence of altered casual capillary glycaemia, suggestivade diabetes mellitus, and its association with socioeconomic, demographic, anthropometric and clinical factors in indigenous women of the United States Brazil.
2	Health quality of life of indigenous women: description of studies carried out between 2009 and 2013.	NETO, R.O.N.; SILVA, G. M.	2014	Portuguese/ Brazil	Description of scientific articles on women's health and quality of life indigenous.
3	User access	GOMES, S. C.;	2017	Portuguese/ Brazil	Evaluate user access

	indigenous people to the services of health Cuiabá, Mato Grosso, Brazil	HOPEFUL, M. A.			indigenous services MEDIA HEALTH ealta complexities of the Municipality of Cuiabá, Mato Grosso, Brazil, from the Indigenous Health Centre (CASAI)
4	Reinventing feminism: Indigenous women and their gender demands	PINTO, A. A.	2010	Portuguese/ Brazil	He had described indigenous issue since perspective gender/ethnicity, seeking to know the political and cultural practices which in this last time have been developing some women's sectors in the labour market. indigenous movement with the support of third sector organisations and society
5	Health and indigenous peoples in Brazil: reflections from the *First*	COIMBRA, C. Jr.	2014	Portuguese/ Brazil	Characterising the nutritional status of women between 14 and 49 years of age and children under

	Health Nutrition Indigenous				of five, based on a probabilistic sample representative of the indigenous population residing in villages in four macro-regions of the country, namely: North, Northeast, Centre-West and South/Southeast.
6	Mortality differentials between indigenous and non-indigenous people indigenous people in Brazilwith based on the 2010 *Demographic*	CAMPOS, M.B.; BORGES, G. M.; QUEIROZ, B. L.; SANTOS, R. V.	2017	Portuguese/ Brazil	Communicate present mortality estimates for indigenous and non-indigenous people in different groups of deities , based on data from the 2010 *Demographic Census.*
7	Reproductive health and indigenous women of the Upper Rio Negro	AZEVEDO, M.	2009	Portuguese/ Brazil	Descrevere describe own conceptions of indigenous women of the Upper Rio Negro on reproductive health, relating them to fertility indicators.

| 8 | Making it visible invisible. Gender-based and intergenerational violence in the world comunidad indígena colombiana/ Making visible the invisible. Gender-based and intergenerational violence in an indigenous Colombian community | DELGADO, F.L.Y.; ENRÍQUEZ, C. H. | 2010 | Spanish/ Colombia | Evaluarla problem of violence gender and between generations in unresguardo Embera indigenous people /Assess the problem of violence in the region gender and intergenerational Embera indigenous reservation. |

After analysing all the articles, it can be observed that the largest number of publications on the subject were between 2009 and 2017. In the years 2010, 2014 and 2017 each of these years with two articles.

The first article was a cross-sectional study with 385 indigenous women, where it was evident that around 70% of indigenous women were obese and overweight, 40% at high risk for cardiovascular disease, more than 30% had stage I hypertension onwards. In addition to being clear that the number of women with DM was much higher than the national rate, being a major concern, many of these women did not use medication, making the risks of complications in the future even greater, the lack of adherence to treatment is a major problem, but sedentary lifestyle (causing overweight and obesity), family history. The indigenous population of Dourados needs monitoring to prevent the occurrence of metabolic disorders and complications related to hyperglycaemia, as well as behavioural modifications with the help of educational interventions.

The second article was an integrative review, where the articles should address the theme of indigenous women's health, between the years 2009 and 2013, most of the articles related to are related to breast cancer, cervix and cytopathological exams, on anaemia in indigenous pregnant women, in addition to the prevention of STIs (Sexually Transmitted Infections).

The third article was a case study on indigenous users' access to health services in Cuiabá, based on documentary analysis, *on-site* observation at the Indigenous Health House (CASAI) in Cuiabá and interviews with key informants. This article shows how access is for the indigenous population where 45% of Indians find it satisfactory, but when it comes to qualifying it was classified as satisfactory, due to the difficulty of Indians in adhering to treatments, due to the lack of knowledge and information they do not have about pathologies.

The fourth article is a bibliographic review of historical data of indigenous women around the world, this study reports all the stories of violence against indigenous women such as: genital mutilation, psychological violence, sexual violence (because of wars or marriage), racial discrimination, in addition to the belief that indigenous women are promiscuous. When they go to the health service they are victims of prejudice due to lack of knowledge.

The fifth article deals with the national meeting on the protection and promotion of their rights. An affirmative action agenda for indigenous women in Brazil. It is about observing and discussing public policies and indigenous women in society, it is an anthropological view of the application of Brazilian laws in relation to women and their culture.

The sixth article is about describing deaths in the Brazilian indigenous population, demographic census explains the difficulty of describing these deaths, mainly due to the cultural aspect. Children are the main focus, and the female sex is approached as the highest rate of deaths.

The seventh article is a qualitative approach to the reproductive health of indigenous women along with fertility rates, women residing in the upper Rio Negro, is a qualitative approach to the reproductive health of indigenous women. analysed their knowledge about their body, sexuality. Observing their traditions in relation to sexuality.

The eighth article is an investigative approach to participatory action orientated by a pespistemiologica

When researching a topic that is always addressed, but never really able to treat and care for this people, due to their culture and belief is quite a challenge. The indigenous people will always prefer to treat pathologies acquired through herbs, rituals or other types of beliefs.

In the health of indigenous women, it is always more delicate and complicated to demonstrate the care and treatment they should follow to improve their quality of life. The lack of adherence in some aspects is evident and the further the indigenous tribe is removed from civilisation, the more complicated it is to adhere to the treatment of chronic pathologies, preventive examinations, adherence to customs that would improve their health, such as the use of condoms to avoid sexually transmitted infections (STIs) among other diseases[7] .

And this does not occur only in Brazil according to studies it is possible to find this in countries such as the United States, Colombia, Peru, Chile, the indigenous tribes of these countries are extremely complicated to carry out traditional medicine care, most prefer the care of their tribe[7] .

The problems of race, health, of making the indigenous woman inferior to the indigenous man came along with the colonising society, with this the Indians began to become poorer and poorer and more isolated[10] .

Indigenous health care has always been modified. This is because the historical process of social, economic, and environmental changes along with the demographic expansion of the colonisers, causing Indians to lose more space[8] . As the indigenous population has more contact with more developed peoples, chronic non-communicable diseases increase even more.

Indigenous people need more intensive public health care in Brazil and worldwide. Due to the fact that they sometimes think that their culture will solve more than preventive medicine or even curative medicine.

V.   CONCLUSION

It is concluded that the application of public health in indigenous women is focused on the education of the population, taking into account their cultural issues. Its location is one of the obstacles to the adherence of the indigenous population to the health system, that is, the more isolated, the more difficult it is to access, and the closer to peoples with different cultures, the more they are exposed to greater risks, therefore women and indigenous people as a whole need more preventive attention, that is, they need health teams to go to them more often to perform the preventive care that each gender needs.

VI. REFERENCES

ARAÚJO, M. A. da P et al.. Quality in hospital care: analysis of the perception of health workers in a hospital in northern Ceará. *Revista de Administração em Saúde*, v. 10, n. 39, p.73-78, Apr/Jun. 2008.

AZEVEDO, M. Reproductive health and indigenous women of the Upper Rio Negro. 2009. Available at:

< http://www.scielo.br/scielo.php?script=sci_arttext&pid=S0103-49792009000300003&lang=pt>

BERNARDES, AG. "Indigenous health and public policies: alterity and state of exception". *Interface - Comunic., Saúde, Educ.,* v.15, n.36, p.153-64, jan./mar. 2011.

BRAZIL, Constitution (1988). Constitution of the Federative Republic of Brazil of 1988. Brasília: National Congress, 1988. Chapter VIII, Of Indians, Article 231. Available at:<http://www. planalto. gov.br/CCML-03/constituição/Constitui%C3A7 ao. htm>. Accessed on: 28/06/2018.

BRAZIL, Law No. 6.001, of 19 December 1973. Provides for the Statute of the Indian. Available at: <http://www.socioambiental.org/inst/leg/pib.shtm>. Accessed on: 28/06/2018.

BRAZIL, MINISTRY OF HEALTH. Secretariat of Health Surveillance, Department of Health Situation Analysis. *Health Brazil 2007: an analysis of the Health Situation.* Brasília: *Ministry of Health.* 2007.

BRAZIL. Special: Health ensures more protection for women. Brasilia: Ministry of Health, 2009.

BRAZIL. Special: Health ensures more protection for women. Brasilia: *Ministry of Health,* 2009.

BRAZIL. Ministry of Health. Bulletin of Nutritional Deficiencies. 2. ed. Brasília: **Ministry of Health**, 2009.

BRAZIL. Ministry of Health. National Health Foundation - FUNASA. National Policy for the Health Care of Indigenous Peoples. Approved by **Ministry of Health** Ordinance No. 254, of 31 January 2002 (Dou No. 26 - section 1, p. 46 to 49, of 6 February 2002).

BRAZIL. National Policy for Comprehensive Women's Health Care: Principles and Guidelines. Brasília: Ministry of Health; 2004.

CAMPOS, M.B.; BORGES, G. M.; QUEIROZ, B. L.; SANTOS, R. V. Mortality differentials between indigenous and non-indigenous people in Brazil based on the 2010 *Demographic Census*. 2017. Available at:< https://scielosp.org/scielo.php?script=sci_arttext&pid=S0102-311X2017000606001&lang=en >.

BRAZILIAN CENTRE FOR ANALYSIS AND PLANNING. Situational Diagnosis of the Indigenous Health Subsystem. **Initial Report** (Revised), São Paulo, 2009. Available at: <http://www.funasa.gov.br/internet/arquivos/vigisus/vigModSsi_DiagnosticoSSI.pdf>. Accessed on 23/06/2018.

COIMBRA, C. Jr. Health and indigenous peoples in Brazil: reflections from the First National Survey of Indigenous Health and Nutrition. 2014.   Available at: <https://scielosp.org/scielo.php?script=sci_arttext&pid=S0102-311X2014000400855&lang=pt>.

COSTA, FAS; *et al.* "Popular practices in indigenous health and integration between scientific and popular knowledge: integrative review". *SANARE, Sobral* - V.15 n.02, p.112-119, Jun./Dec. - 2016.

CRUZ, K.R. Indigenous peoples and health policy in Brazil: the specific and the differentiated as challenges. Dissertation (Master in Public Policy) - Federal University of Maranhão, São Luís, 2003. Accessed on 27/11/2017.

DELGADO, F.L.Y.; ENRÍQUEZ, C. H. Haciendo visible lo invisible. Violencia de género y entre generaciones en una comunidad indígena colombiana. 2010. Available at: <http://www.scielo.org.co/scielo.php?script=sci_arttext&pid=S0120-

53072010000300015&lang=en>.

FREITAS, G.A; SOUZA, M.C.C.; LIMA, R.C. Prevalence of diabetes mellitus and associated factors in indigenous women from the municipality of Dourados, Mato Grosso do Sul, Brazil. 2016. Available at:<https://scielosp.org/scielo.php?script=sci_arttext&pid=S0102-311X2016000805010&lang=en>.

FUNAI. 2014. Indigenous Women participate in National Meeting on the Protection and Promotion of their Rights. 19 Nov. Available at http://www.funai. gov.br/index.php/comunicacao/noticias/2223- -mulheres-indigenas-participam-de-encontro-   nacional-a-protecao-e-promocao-dos-seus-d direitos, accessed 7/10/2017;

NATIONAL HEALTH FOUNDATION (Brazil). *Basic and specialised care for indigenous peoples: regulation of incentives*. Brasília, DF. 2007.

NATIONAL HEALTH FOUNDATION (FUNASA). *Informative Bulletin n.1/2006*. Brasília, DF, 2006

NATIONAL HEALTH FOUNDATION (FUNASA). Available at: <www.funasa.gov.br>. Accessed on 23/06/2018.

NATIONAL HEALTH FOUNDATION (FUNASA). *Morbimortality Report* 2002. Brasília: DF, 2003.

GOMES, S. C.; ESPERIDIÃO, M.A. Access of indigenous users to health services in Cuiabá, Mato Grosso,   Brazil.   2017.   Available   at: <https://scielosp.org/scielo.php?script=sci_arttext&pid=S0102311X2017000605010&lang=p>.

GUIMARÃES, VLB. "The quality of indigenous health care in Brazil". Oswaldo Cruz Foundation. **AGGEU Magalhães Research Centre - CpqAM**. Specialisation course in public health. Recife. 2011.

KABAD, JF; PÍCOLI, RP; ARANTES, R. The health of the indigenous family. **Ed. UFMS**. Optional Module 2 - Post-Graduation in Primary Care in Family Health. 2011.

MENDES, K.D.S.; SILVEIRA, R.C.C.P.; GALVÃO, C.M. Integrative review: research method for the incorporation of evidence in health and nursing. Texto Contexto- Enferm. v.17, n.4, 2008.

NETO, R. O. N.; SILVA, G. M. Health and quality of life of indigenous women: description of works carried out between 2009 and 2013. 2014.

NETO, RON; SILVA, GM. "Health and quality of life of indigenous women: description of studies carried out between 2009 and 2013".

PAGLIARO, H; AZEVEDO, H. "Reproductive behaviour of indigenous peoples in Brazil, interface between demography and anthropology. In: Wong LR, organiser". **Población y salud sexual y reproductiva em América Latina**. Rio de Janeiro: Série Investigaciones; 2008. p. 41533.

PAGLIARO, H; AZEVEDO, MM; SANTOS, RV. Demography of Indigenous Peoples in Brazil: a critical overview. Rio de Janeiro: **Editora Fiocruz and Brazilian Association of Population Studies/Abep**, 2005.

PEREIRA, ER et al. "Sexual and reproductive health and sociocultural aspects of indigenous women". **Rev Bras Promoç Saúde**, Fortaleza, 27(4): 445-454, Oct./Dec., 2014.

PINTO, A. A. Reinventing feminism: Indigenous women and their gender demands. 2010.

SALES, JM. "Bioethics and gender violence of indigenous peoples: diagnosis of a negligence". **University of Brasilia**. Faculty of Health Sciences - Postgraduate Programme in bioethics. Brasília. 2016.

SANTOS, R. V. et al. Health of Indigenous Peoples and Public Policies in Brazil. In: GIOVSNELLA, et al. Políticas e Sistema de Saúde no Brasil. Rio de Janeiro: **Editora Fiocruz**,. 2008. p.33-55.

SEGATO, Rita Laura. 2003. An affirmative action agenda for indigenous women in Brazil. Anthropology Series, n. 326. Brasília: Department of Anthropology/ University of Brasília (UnB). Available at: www.agende.org.br/docs/File/dados_pesquisas/outros/Acoes%20para%20mulheres%20indigenas. pdf. [accessed on 08/10/2017].

SILVA, HB; DIAZ, CMG; SILVA, KF. "The culture and health of indigenous women: integrative review". *Revista de pesquisa cuidado é fundamental Online*. 2015. oct./dez. 7(4): 31753184. ISSN 2175-5361. DOI: 10.9789/2175-5361.2015.v7i4.3175-3184

TANAKA, OY; ESPÍRITO SANTO, ACG. "Evaluation of the quality of primary care using childhood respiratory disease as a tracer, in a health district of the municipality of São Paulo". *Revista Brasileira de Saúde Materno Infantil*, Recife. v. 8, n. 3, p. 325-332, jul. / sep. 2008.

VERANI, C. B. L. The Indian Health Policy and the Organisation of Health Services. 2011. Available at: <http://sis.funasa.gov.br/portal/publicacoes/pub705.rtf>. Accessed on: 27/06/2018.

Printed by Books on Demand GmbH, Norderstedt / Germany